WHALES AND ETHICS

Please Return to

NDCS
19a James St west
Bath
Avon
BA1 2BT

Whales and Ethics

Proceedings from Whales and Ethics,
a seminar hosted by the Fisheries Research Institute
in collaboration with Survival in the High North.

Edited by
Örn D. Jónsson.

Fisheries Research Institute
University of Iceland
University Press

Acknowledgement:

Fynn Lynge's paper which was submitted at the conference at the Fisheries Research Institute in Reykjavík, May 1991, is going to appear as a subchapter in his book *Animal Wars—an Arctic Perspective* to be published by the University Press of New England, Hannover, New Hampshire, USA, towards the end of 1992. By courtesy of the publishers, it is printed here in its final version before the publication of the book.

ISBN 9979-54-035-4

University Press, University of Iceland
Sudurgata, 101 Reykjavík, Iceland

Contents

Opening Remarks

GÍSLI PÁLSSON

Department of Social Anthropology

University of Iceland

I welcome you to this event, which is jointly organized by the Fisheries Research Institute at this University and Survival in the High North. The meeting focuses on the question "Is it right to hunt whales?". Whaling is a hot political issue in many countries, including Iceland. And hot political debates should always be matched by a great deal of objective reflection and scholarly discussion; this is essential in a democratic society where people like to think they are well informed and that they ought to make rational decisions about their lives. It would, admittedly, be somewhat naive and simplistic to claim full independence for the academic world, to present science as an enterprise totally removed from the social context to which it belongs. After all, scientific work is always shaped by social context. Absolute standards of objectivity and neutrality, may therefore be difficult to define. It would be quite dangerous, on the other hand, to go to the other extreme and deny the scholarly pursuit any degree of independence; to relegate the quest for knowledge to the Ministry of Truth; we know too many lessons from totalitarian regimes.

One of the aims of the Fisheries Research Institute at this university is to provide a context for open-minded and rational discourse on resource management and environmental issues, a discourse as free as possible from ideological constraints and political forces. The institute has already arranged important public meetings on fisheries management in Iceland.

Three distinguished scholars are to give talks at our meeting today. They are: Margaret Klinowska, who has carried out extensive research on mammalian ecology at Cambridge University, Milton Freeman, who has studied indigenous hunters and gatherers in the Canadian Arctic for years, and Finn Lynge, a theologian who has long experience of fishing communities in Polar regions. The organizers have invited several other people, known for their opposition to whaling, to speak here—including Robin Barstow, spokesman for Cetacean Society International, and one representative from Greenpeace International. They have also invited two American lawyers, Anthony D'Amato and Sudhir Choptra, who have recently argued in academic journals for the legal concept of animal rights. These persons however have had to reject the invitation to address this meeting because of other commitments. This is rather unfortunate, as their participation would, no doubt, have enriched our discussions.

The main question on the agenda, "Is it right to hunt whales?", is not a novel topic in Western society. Recently, however, environmental debates, including the debate on whaling, has taken a dramatic turn in many countries—and internationally, as all of you are well aware of; indeed the emphasis on the global context is one of the peculiar characteristics of modern environmental discourse. Over the last two centuries or so, the inhabitants of the industrialized world have often presented themselves as masters of their environments, as godly beings removed from nature and accountable only to themselves. We need not elaborate on the tragic consequences of this primitive, anthropocentric and expansionist world-view. Nowadays, in contrast, people increasingly think of themselves as part of nature along with other animals, including sea mammals. In this latter view, humans have a particular responsibility not only to other humans but also to members of other species, to fellow inhabitants of the animal kingdom. Whaling, then, ceases to be merely "economic production", the extraction of "resources" or lumps of energy from the sea. Some of the key issues of environmental discussion in coming years are likely to focus around ethical questions, such as human responsibility and on animal rights.

Just as the scientific enterprise is inevitably shaped by the society in which it occurs, environmental discussions are necessarily rooted in their times. It is important, therefore, for environmentalists as well as for academics (whether they be environmentalists or not) to step back from time to time and evaluate the state of affairs. Such a re-evaluation raises complex issues and exceedingly difficult questions. Rather than avoid complex issues and difficult questions, however, we should confront them with frankness and honesty. The present meeting has been organized in that spirit.

Ethics of a Killer Whale

FINN LYNGE

Consultant in Greenland Affairs

Danish Foreign Ministry

Nobody who has followed the whaling/anti-whaling debate over the last few years can be in doubt: as the IWC Scientific Committee is capable of documenting more and more whale stocks to be good in health, and as the work on a revised set of management procedures for a resumed whaling activity is nearing its completion, the anti-whaling lobby leans increasingly toward a moral line of reasoning: whales are intelligent and sentient, they are wonderful and very special creatures, and it is quite simply immoral to kill them. A whole new series of arguments are being built up for the purpose of exempting whales from the general regime of sustainable use of nature's resources. And we are all being told to stop thinking of humans as something special: whales too are uniquely special, and we should beware of thinking along the lines of traditional anthropocentric morality.

This new line of thinking is a challenge to traditional ethics. In the Western and Mid-Eastern world—Mosaic, Christian, Islamic—it is presupposed that biological life appears in two categories: 1) humankind, and 2) all the rest. Humans alone are made in the image of God.

In a Darwinistic perspective, this conveys the picture of biological life as a continuum, but with built-in mutations which lift up the stage of life unto different and still higher levels, progressively. With the awakening of consciousness of the self, combined with the ability to speak, the human being became the first and so far the only animal capable of pointing his finger, saying *you* and *I*. Thereby humans reached a stage of life essentially different from all other life manifestations. The foundation was laid for a conscious individuation process inside the species of *Homo sapiens*.

For all other animal species, survival mechanisms are geared—in the end—to the survival of the group, the population, the species. In situations of stress, most vertebrate animals fend for themselves and their progeny, obviously with no thought for the species, and this is how the interests of the species are served. But no animals other than the humans have passed the threshold of individuation, where, in situations of stress, the interest of the individual can be brought to militate against those of the group.

With the advent of *Homo sapiens*, a new level of evolution was reached when it became reasonable and proper to start caring consciously for the individual, indeed in some respects valuing the individual above all—the individual *Homo sapiens*, that is. But not the individuals of other animal species.

Historically, this phenomenon has been most apparent in the thought of the great religious personalities throughout the ages—all stressing the immense value of each single human person. In recent times, as we know, this idea has received collective and societal support with the French Revolution, the American Declaration of Independence and—in our times—the UN Charter of Human Rights.

Humans are the only animals to make the distinction between good and evil, and—as opposed to other kinds of animals—humans are continuously exploring all possible facets and extremes of both good and evil, putting acceptable behavioural codes to a constant test. We will always have among us a Dr. Mengele and a Mother Theresa. This doesn't go on without a lot of noise, involving both heroism and tragedy. Only humans are capable of heroism and tragedy on an individual, personal basis. We are restless and probing, and unlike other animals we are obviously ill at ease with ourselves, capable of behaving humanely as well as inhumanely. It is no foregone conclusion that we are at harmony with our inner selves.

Not so the other animals. There is no evidence whatever that they should feel anything like remorse when hunting and killing one another. They know no good and evil: they are innocent. No whale can exhibit "unwhalely behaviour"—not even a killer whale. On this score, a whale is like any other animal. This is part of the simplicity and the beauty of the animal world, this is part of what makes inhumane treatment of animals so unbearable: when abused, they are not only defenceless, they are quintessientially innocent victims of the evil whims or greed of humankind.

In our part of the world, this has, for millenia, been the fundamental view on the law-making concerning rights and duties that is centred on human beings.

Is this view becoming obsolete?

Granted, we have in front of us, every day, everywhere here in the West, evidence of a caricature of the Mosaic-Christian model of the animals' role: the human being on top of creation, and with the—legally—unchallenged right to destroy animal habitats, wage unnecessarily cruel wars against pest animals, toxify the food chains and enslave so-called domestic animals by the millions, if not billions, in view of industrialized execution—in other words, seemingly unlimited abuse.

Then, in all fairness, we also have many examples of responsible and reasonable management of animal life, whether domestic or wild.

But the fact remains that animals do have problems with humans—bad problems.

Obviously, there are two ways one can attack this issue: either by stressing *our duty as humans* to behave ethically vis-à-vis the animals, or by starting to talk about *the right of animals* to be treated reasonably.

The first kind of approach to the problem is consonant with traditional Western thought. According to the best of this tradition, we cannot just heedlessly destroy the animal habitats or inflict wanton loss and suffering. We have an obligation to treat creation right. Whether we like it or not, we are in actual fact stewards of the natural environment of which we are the masters.

Over and against this view, another concept is now emerging: that of animals having their own rights. Humans are not that special after all, it is said, and have no reason to feel conceited. Biological life is a continuum from the least evolved form to the highest. If we think that humans have the right to live in as far as possible without suffering, we must perforce extend that right also to species other than our own, in as much as they, too, are capable of pain. Any creature capable of pain has a right not to be subjected to unnecessary suffering. Any talk about a special ethical prerogative in favour of humans is not only nonsense, it is an especially foul kind of species-based narrow-mindedness and chauvinism, it is *speciesism*. Peter Singer, the Australian philosopher who has fathered most of the contemporary animal liberation thinking, mentions the theoretical example of a medical experiment that must be performed on an living animal. If the scientist in charge has access to a mentally retarded person, the experiment could just as well be performed on her/him rather on a healthy, sentient rat.[1]

One point in this line of reasoning, however, is not properly elucidated. In the ethical standards governing our day-to-day behaviour, rights are intimately connected with duties. If you have a human right to democracy, then you also have an obligation—a moral obligation, not necessarily a juridical one—to behave democratically yourself. If you have the right to know the truth, you also have the duty to be truthful yourself.

1 Peter Singer: *Animal Liberation.* English Edition: Thorsons Publishers Limited, Wellingborough Northamptonshire, 1975. American edition: Avon books, New York 1975.

He argues that no such experiment can be justifiable at all "unless it is so important that the use of a retarded human being would also be justifiable." Avon ed., p. 78.

If the animals have their rights, what are their duties?

Does it make sense to talk this way in the first place? Duties presuppose an ethical standard. Do animals have ethics? What are the ethics of a killer whale?

Clearly, this question is devoid of meaning. Animals can have no obligations in an ordinary sense of the word. They make no moral choices.[2] They are simple and innocent and at peace with themselves, even when they hunt and kill one another. If you want to attribute the concept of "right" to animals which intrinsically and at all times are incapable of assuming "duties", then the word "right" assumes a different meaning. Presumably, then

2   At this point, one may object that also in the human realm, we have important instances where rights are dissociated from duties. One obvious example of this is the human predicament of helplessness at the beginning and
the end of life. Infants enjoy the protection of human rights, but have no
duties.   The same goes for senile inmates of an old folks' home.
Conclusion: it is possible, in some case even right and proper, to dissociate
rights from duties. Duties furthermore appear as a more narrow concept
than rights. If we can accept rights without duties in humans, we surely
also should accept it in whales.

   Nobody, though, can deny that the state of an infant and a senile person
represents the exception to the rule, which is the intimate association of
rights and duties characteristic of responsibility.   The human person is
essentially the responsible animal which experiences first an ascent, later a
decline of the capacity for taking responsibility. This ascent and decline of
maturity with its blurring or suspension of the characteristic of which clearly is an accountability, which is unique to Homo sapiens. In the human,
we can accept instances of rights with duties. The infant and the senile
person have their human rights because they are going to exercise, or have
exercised, a kind of accountability, which no other animal is capable of
showing at any point of its life span.

   The case of the mentally ill or retarded person is not much different. It is
true that there are many persons who are excused from the otherwise normal duties in life, while retaining some basic and inalienable rights, such as
the right to life and, under certain circumstances, decent living conditions.
However, trying to construe a set of properties in a healthy and normal
population of one species on the basis of the properties inherent in sick
individuals of a completely different species brings the matter to a point
where the rationality of the argument is hard to take seriously.

the only purpose of this exercise is to translate the whole matter into an obligation for humans to treat animals correctly—an obligation which was there anyway in the first place.

Further down the road, and dealing with whales specifically, we hear that biological life comes in three categories:

1) humans
2) whales
3) all other animals and other biological life.

The whales are a category apart because in the eyes of so many people, they are *uniquely special*.

"Other animals" are all other species placed below humans and whales in the respective food-chains of land and sea.

Maybe this view has been most clearly forwarded by Robbins Barstow.[3] Dr. Barstow doesn't make use of the general animal rights' rhetoric. He argues the cause of the whales and nothing else. As far as the basic relationship between animals and humans goes, Barstow doesn't further any arguments against the sustainable use of nature's resources in general; he makes no distinction between the plant and animal kingdoms, respectively, and thus doesn't promote the vegetarian cause; neither does he argue against a sustainable and ecologically sound harvest of wildlife. His sole concern is the whales, for which he has a deep-seated feeling of wonder and awe. These strong emotions are motivated by a series of reasons—biological, ecological, cul-

3 *"Beyond Whale Species Survival. Peaceful Coexistence and Mutual Enrichment as a Basis for Human/Cetacean Relations."* Sonar. *The Magazine of the Whale and Dolphin Society.* Bath, Avon, U.K.
   No.2, autumn 1989, pg. 10-13.

   Barstow is American. The official New Zealand position in the whaling issue also points in the same direction. At the 3rd session of the Preparatory Committee of the UN Conference on Environment and Development, the New Zealand delegate stated that whales are "in a sense the equivalent in the marine environment of human beings in the land environment." (UNCED Prep. Com., Working group II: item 2. Statement on Cetaceans, p. 12. Geneva, August 12, 1991).

tural, political—which makes him consider the whales as "uniquely special" and therefore exempt from the general regime of sustainable utilization of wildlife as forwarded by the World Conservation Strategy and the Brundtland Commission Report.

Of course whales are a wonder of nature in very many ways, and people are entitled to nurture strong emotions in that connection. It seems, though, that there could be grounds for asking a few counter-questions:

Are these views really as universal as claimed by some? Are they shared by the majority of the more than one billion Chinese, the 650 million people of Africa, the 80 million Arabs? Granted we all know about public opinion in the Anglo-Saxon countries. But can one equate an Anglo-Saxon and—to some extent—West-European trend with a world opinion?

In some countries, respect for an animal and the killing of it go together. In other countries, the two are opposed. For both of these types of cultures, the attitude of the other is incomprehensible.

We all know that the Anglo-Saxon countries have a strong tradition for wanting to export their own cultural pattern and value systems to everybody else, so it comes as no surprise that an essentially western urban phenomenon is presented as "all but universal". It does give rise though, to some questions: if cultures do exist in which respect for an animal and the killing of it go together, are they not entitled to go on existing? If not, what is the ethical reason for liquidating these cultures? If respect for an animal and the killing of it are mutually exclusive, what then is the attitude of the Anglo-Saxon city dwellers to the cows, pigs and chickens in their own slaughter-houses? And what are the ethical grounds for this attitude, presumably one of contempt?

While never doubting for a moment that whales are uniquely special to many people, there is good reason to point out that horses are very special to many other people. Are fewer less people to whom horses are uniquely special than there are people to whom whales assume this role?

To the 670 million hindus of the world, it's the *cow* which is truly special and sacred. Are there more than 670 million people to whom a whale is more special than a cow? Perhaps. It would be interesting to see it documented.

To the Arabs, the most divine of all creatures in the white *gyrfalcon* of the Arctic. They use it for their traditional hunting sports. They have a hard time getting hold of this bird, and they go to great lengths to procure it. In the Arab world one gyrfalcon is surely valued higher than many whales.

Or is if the *eagle*? This fascinating bird has qualified as a symbol of all imperialistic Western empires since the Romans.

Who knows! One thing is certain, however: to very many people around the world , the most uniquely special animal is the *dog.* Humankind's most ancient and faithful friend has been there from pole to pole, on all continents, at all times. The dog is by all counts the most useful, probably the the most time-consuming, and certainly the most beloved of all animals. It lives with us in a symbiosis of unchallenged mutual enrichment, to use the term which Dr. Barstow attributes to the relationship between whales and humans. What would all the lonesome people, the watchmen, the herders what would all the blind people of the world do without a dog? How would the entire Eskimo culture have come about without dogs?

There can be no doubt: the dog is uniquely special of all animals. And yet, in some countries, people eat dogs. In Greenland, we do, occasionally. Is there a serious *ethical* reason for not eating dogs? One which holds water philosophically?

The most serious objection against setting the seventy-nine different whale species apart from the general regime governing animals and people is the fact that different times and different cultural circumstances produce different totem animals. Once you have accepted setting whales apart in a politically different management regime because of your's and your friends' personal emotional preferences, then there is no rational reason in the world to stop at the whales. Other people have *their* feelings for other kinds of animals.

The process is simply bound to slide into the more general animal rights philosophy. The seals, sea lions and sea elephants are surely as brainy and wonderfully adapted to their environment as at least one of the many different whale species, and so they are entitled to a special regime. Otherwise we would be facing some kind of speciesm in favour of whales! If all marine mammals enjoy these special rights, then why not the semi-aquatic animals? If beavers, what about all other furbearers in the woods? Et cetera, et cetera... There is no doubt: if whales have rights, then every other sentient animal in the world with a brain capacity of some kind must have similar rights. Nothing else is philosophically consistent.

It cannot be a matter of moral rights, since animals can't be held morally responsible for anything. It will have to be a question of bestowing juridical rights on animals, their different nature notwithstanding. A political decision will have to be made about the right of animals to the pursuit of life and consonant with their own nature—on par with the Human Rights Declaration of the United Nations.

Astounding as it is, this line of thinking does have its supporters—astounding if for no other reason than because it is completely impossible to put into practice in any other consistent way.

Whatever the animal rights protagonists may put forward in support of their cause, the simple fact remains that all and any value system of any practical use perforce has to be human-centered. It is simply impossible to bestow on animals the same right to live and enjoy the pursuit of happiness as we do on humans. The entire debate over the environment and the relationship between humans and animals is a struggle over space on a crowded planet. People multiply and proliferate from pole to pole like no other large size mammal has ever done, from the mountains to the plains and far out at sea, everywhere. Animals are pushed away or forced into new patterns of ecological balance or imbalance. And we are being forced to a great deal of new thinking about our relationship with nature.

Through all this, one basic fact remains: no human group has ever been ready, so far , to sacrifice part of itself in order to serve the interests of animals in jeopardy. But humans have always been, and presumably always will be ready to sacrifice the lives of animals. This is the people-centered reality, and no responsible authority is about to change that. The world is crowded, and lives, both animal and human, have to be managed; but the difference is that human lives are managed through birth control and family planning, whereas animal population growth which is bothersome to humans is regulated through lethal measures. Anyone wanting to build a workable ethic for the relationship between humans and animals will have to take this simple fact into account, if for no other reason than because it is not likely to be changed in any foreseeable future. Pest control is not unethical; on the contrary: it is clearly a moral act to curb the proliferation of disease-carrying rodents, just to take one obvious example. In any big city in the world, this control takes place by the constant and unceasing killing of millions and millions of rats by slow-working poison. Any big city is built upon an horrendous sea of suffering of this intelligent and sentient, family-loving, yet so unfortunate, animal species. That is a terrible thought, yet true. But it is not unethical. It is a necessity.

Animal ethics will always be people-centered, for two reasons:
– ethics originate in the human mind, man alone having a moral choice, and
– in a situation of conflict, human life will be preferred over animal life.

Once that has been said, there is every good reason to repeat what has been said already: that we are obliged to treat our fellow creatures right, protect their habitats, combat contamination of the environment, prevent harassment of the animals, and avoid unnecessary cruelty in wildlife management and harvest practices. Humans must care.

Animals have no responsibility for good or bad. They have no ethical standard. The killer whale does no evil when it teaches its young ones how to play cat-&-mouse with a stunned sea lion, or when it tears up an intensely suffering, defenceless humpback whale and starts eating its tongue without bothering to kill it first. This is the cruel order of nature, and that cruelty is not evil. The killer whale is innocent.

We are not innocent. We are responsible. Killing animals can be legitimate, even necessary. But to us, wanton cruelty is evil. Unlike animals, we do know concepts like love of our fellow creatures, and compassion.

We are under an obligation to care.

Brains, Behaviour and Intelligence in Cetaceans

(Whales, Dolphins and Porpoises)

MARGARET KLINOWSKA

Research Group in Mammalian Ecology and Reproduction,
Physiological Laboratory, Cambridge University

Introduction

It is widely believed that cetaceans (the whales, dolphins and porpoises) are highly "intelligent". Probably the major historical basis for this dogma is the size and complex surface appearance of cetacean brains (Figure 1). The idea that brain size and surface characteristics are related to "intelligence" was widespread among neuroanatomists around the turn of the century, but received a severe blow when it was found that the brains of several distinguished people (who had bequeathed their bodies to science) showed no outstanding characteristics whatever and were, in fact, disappointingly ordinary (Kuhlenbeck, 1978). This was just as well, as elements of such work were being badly misused to justify repressive racist, anti-feminist and colonial attitudes. The subject remained generally out of fashion until John Lilly, a medical doctor by training, became impressed by the absolute size of cetacean brains. His famous book "Mind in the Waters" (Lilly, 1967) appears to have led to much of the modern interest in this topic.

We all know in a general way what we mean by "intelligence" but unfortunately, it is so difficult to define strictly that, even when it comes to devising comparative tests for humans, all kinds of problems arise. The problems in defining "intelligence" in such a way that valid comparisons can be made across a wide of range of species have yet to be overcome, although this has not deterred a great deal of research into the subject.

Brain Quantity

Size

If "intelligence" was simply determined by absolute brain size, there would be no difficulty in deciding which species was top (Table 1). But as the species with the biggest brains also tend to be the ones with the biggest bodies, it might be that large animals just need larger brains to control and maintain their larger bodies. Even when we talk of "intelligence" in a general way, we mean something more than the sum of body control systems. A simple way to make allowance for different body weights is to express brain weight as a percentage of body weight (Table 2). In this list humans are seen to have a great advantage over the others, and we also have a very different view of the large whales. Of course, these are only very limited lists to illustrate this type of approach to the problem.

Species	Brain weight (approx.) grams	Body weight (approx.) tonnes
Sperm whale (male)	7,820	37.00
African elephant	7,500	5.00
Fin whale	6,930	90.00
Killer whale	5,620	6.00
Bottlenose dolphin	1,600	0.17
Human	1,500	0.07
Cow	500	0.6

Table 1. Approximate brain weights and body weights of some mammals, in order of brain weight.

Species	Brain weight as % of body weight
Human	2.10
Bottlenose dolphin	0.94
African elephant	0.15
Killer whale	0.09
Cow	0.08
Sperm whale (male)	0.02
Fin whale	0.01

Table 2. Approximate brain weights as a percentage of approximate body weights of some mammals.

Researchers have made far more extensive and sophisticated attempts to investigate comparative intelligence in this way. There is, however, a basic problem in compiling lists of this type, and that is deciding which weights to take as typical of a species. For example, normal humans can have brains weighing anything between 900 and 2,000 grams. The weight of an individual brain will also vary depending on whether it is fresh or preserved, and on exactly which parts are included. Body weight varies greatly between individuals, and in some whale species the weight of individual animals can vary by about 40% over a year because of their seasonal feeding habits. The brain weight to body weight relationship varies with age—young mammals have proportionally smaller bodies and larger heads, and brain size decreases significantly in old age. There can be marked sex differences in body size, for example adult female baleen whales in many species are much larger than males, while in sperm whales it is the adult males which are much larger than the females. Normal variations in brain and body size have only been well studied in a few species, and usually a researcher seeking to compile extensive brain and body weight lists has no choice but to take whatever specimens are available, regardless of whether the material is really representative of the species as a whole.

Some of the most extensive modern comparative studies have been made by Jerison (e.g. 1978), who has developed an index, the encephalization quotient (EQ), to express the brain weight/body weight relationship. His studies do show some cetaceans (e.g. toothed whales like the killer whale and sperm whale) with an EQ similar to humans. However, other studies conclude that relative brain size is not necessarily related to "intelligence". Pilleri, Gihr and Kraus (1985) made an exhaustive study of rodent brain size in relation to behaviour and concluded that "intelligence", whether human or animal, is not a unified brain function, but one which is too complex to be characterised with a single numerical index. They found that cerebral quotients (various ways of expressing relative brain and body size) are generally inconclusive as criteria for mammalian "intelligence".

Macphail (1982), in an extensive review of brain and behaviour in vertebrates, also found that brain size and characteristics were unsatisfactory indicators of "intelligence", because there are too many anomalies. A particular example is the spiny anteater (an egg laying mammal, related to the duck-billed platypus), with a neocortex (the so-called 'modern' part of the brain, which is greatly developed in primates and humans) relatively much larger than that of a human. Despite this endowment, nobody has so far put forward any claims for superior "intelligence" in spiny anteaters. Another problem with the search for a comparative measure of "intelligence" through brain quantity is addressed in the volume edited by Hahn, Jensen and Dudek (1979). Although a number of the papers deal with laboratory species selected and bred for increased brain size, there is extraordinary difficulty in demonstrating any improvement in performance on a variety of tests either within or between species.

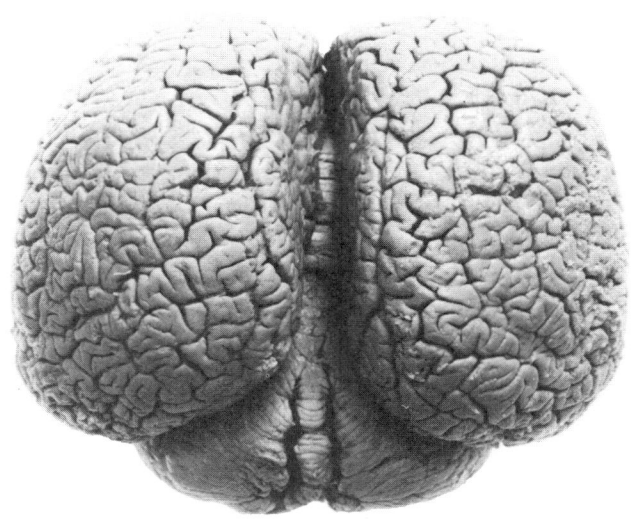

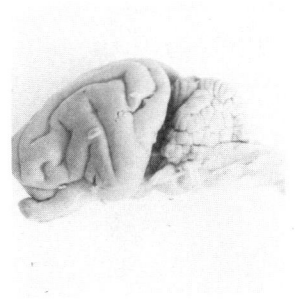
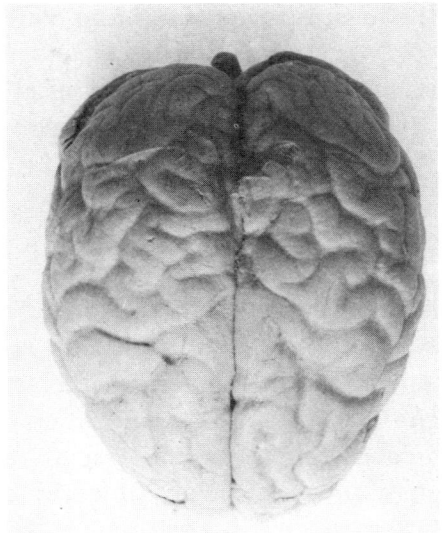

Figure 1. Brains of (top) common dolphin and (right) chimpanzee (viewed from above), and (left) of cat (viewed from the left side). All reproduced to the same scale.

Appearance

The degree of convolution or folding of the cortical brain surface has often in the past been taken as an absolute indicator of "intelligence". However, more recent work regards this as simply a mechanical reflection of an increase in neocortical volume. Jerison (1979), for example, regards degree of convolution and absolute brain size as equivalent measures, speculating that the extra volume is required to accommodate increasingly complex connections between the brain cells. Ridgway (1986) presents evidence from a variety of sources to show that bottlenose dolphins have a much higher index of folding than humans. However, as Ridgway (1986) also explains, the neocortex of the cetacean brain is relatively thin—about half that of humans— giving a total average dolphin neocortical volume about 80% of that of humans. Also, as explained in more detail below, cetacean neocortical structure is generally very much simpler than that of land mammals, and does not therefore conform to the assumptions that more convoluted neocortices are necessarily more voluminous or more complex. This is not the only anomaly; for example compare the convoluted appearances of the horse and chimpanzee brains.

Brain Quality

Another school of thought (e.g. Holloway, 1979), finds the consideration of brain and body sizes alone insufficient, indeed "trivial", and emphasises the importance of the evolutionary changes in brain organisation. Holloway (1979) goes on to demonstrate that brain weight is a poor predictor of the internal structural complexity which he believes to be the most important factor in the evolution of "intelligence".

Studies of the internal structure of carefully preserved dolphin brains using a variety of techniques (e.g. Kesarev, Malofeyeva and Trykova, 1977; Morgane, Jacobs and

Galaburda, 1986; Garey and Revishchin, 1990; Glazer, Morgane and Leranth, 1990) show that these animals have not developed the latest stage of brain evolution, characteristic of land mammals. It is thought that this line of evolution began about 50 million years ago in land mammals, whereas the cetacean ancestors returned to the water some 70 million years ago, well before this stage was reached. Although the cetacean brain has not followed the course of evolution of the land mammals, it does retain all the conservative characteristics seen in primitive land forms, such as hedgehogs and bats. The dolphin brain shows none of the anatomical structural heterogeneity characteristic of more evolved brains such as those of primates, but the regions of the neocortex can be differentiated by electrophysiological methods, and are arranged in very much the same order as in the hypothetical ancestor of mammals (Supin, Mukhametov, Ladygina, Popov, Mass and Poliakova, 1978).

The neocortex is the part of the brain which most clearly differentiates mammals from non-mammals, and there is a wide belief that the growth of the neocortex is responsible for the evolution of "intelligence". The anatomical characteristics of mammalian neocortex are that it has six layers and that different functional areas (e.g. that dealing with vision) have somewhat different organisation of these layers. The anatomical studies cited above demonstrate that cetaceans only have five layers in the neocortex (layer IV is missing) and that there is no anatomically different organisation of these layers according to function. In some views (e.g. Kesarev *et al.*, 1977) this means that cetaceans have no true neocortex, or only a pre-neocortex. If a neocortex is really essential for the development of "intelligence", cetaceans are clearly disqualified. However, Macphail (1982) comprehensively demolishes the idea of a special role for the neocortex in "intelligence".

Behaviour

In the laboratory

Yet another school of thought believes that the significance of the relative size or structural complexity of brains needs to be validated by behavioural data before any assumptions can be made about their role in the development of "intelligence". While a variety of laboratory tasks have been used, that of learning set formation (the inter-problem improvement in performance seen in subjects given a series of discriminations involving different pairs of stimuli) has been widely explored since Harlow (1949) concluded that the results reflected evolutionary relationships.

Unfortunately, subsequent work showed that closely related species may have widely divergent performances, and that some "lower" species may equal or excel "higher" species. Further, the ordering of species does not agree with that predicted from relative brain size (EQ) (Table 3). Macphail (1982) remarks that it is not clear that any of the differences in performance in learning set formation (or any of the other types of behavioural studies considered) observed are due to differences in intellectual capacity, and he cites a number of studies which demonstrate, as might be expected, that relative species performance is very dependent on details of experimental technique.

Species	Score % (trial 2)	Encephalization quotient (EQ)	Order
Langur	98	1.29	primate
Mink	95	? (1–1.5)*	carnivore
Ferret	90	? (1–1.5)*	carnivore
Bottlenose dolphin	87	5.31	cetacean
Rhesus monkey	86	2.09	primate
Cat	70	1.71	carnivore
Rat	60	0.40	rodent
Squirrel	60	1.10	rodent

Table 3. Learning set formation (data from various sources cited by Macphail, 1982).

* exact EQ not available, therefore these species have been given the general carnivore EQ range.

Communication

While all non-human animals have ways of communicating with each other, for example by body language, sounds, touch or chemicals, they have not developed anything of comparable versatility to human language. Although many attempts have been made, no non-human has yet been taught more than the rudiments of human-type language. Macphail (1982) describes the experiments and species (chimpanzee, gorilla, bottlenose dolphin, California sea lion, pigeon) concerned, and argues that such performances to date are better described as ordering responses sequentially for reward, rather than as real steps on the road to language. He also puts forward an interesting interpretation of the human capacity for problem solving, which is quite beyond the capacity of any non-human. If humans solve problems, directly or indirectly, with the aid of language, the superiority of humans in problem solving might simply reflect the possession of language, and the capacity for language, in turn might be a species-specific specialisation, independent of general "intelligence".

Discussion

Clearly, the cetacean type of mammalian brain is sufficient for the purpose, but it is anatomically simple and lacks the new structures which are conventionally associated with the development of "intelligence" among land mammals. However, as we have seen, there are good reasons for questioning these conventions.

Dolphin brains are relatively large, but again there are reasons for questioning the assumption that brain size is related to "intelligence". Crick and Mitchison's (1983) theory of the function of dream sleep may provide an alternative explanation for such anomalously large brains. They propose that rapid-eye-movement sleep (REM or dream or paradoxical sleep) acts to remove undesirable interactions in networks of cells in the cerebral cortex. They call this process, which is the opposite of learning, but different from forgetting, "reverse learning". Animals which cannot use this system need another way to avoid overloading the neural network, for example by having bigger brains. The spiny anteater and dolphins are the only mammals so far tested which do not have REM sleep (Allison, Van Twyner and Goff, 1972; Mukhametov, 1984)—and they also have disproportionally large brains. So, following this line of reasoning, dolphins and spiny anteaters would have to have big brains because they cannot dream.

The behaviour of dolphins is frequently cited as evidence for high "intelligence". The capacity of some smaller cetacean species (not all—see Defran and Pryor, 1980) to learn performance tricks in captivity is often taken as "proof" of cetacean intelligence, but many other animals—from elephants to fleas—can achieve such feats, without this being taken as evidence for a special order of "intelligence". People who have been in close contact with dolphins and whales often speak of a feeling that they are with an "intelligent" animal, but many dog-

[margin handwritten notes:] Nb: REM theory Pocket brain also attributed to removal of stimulus prior to birth.

owners, for example, have a close rapport with their pets and also speak of "intelligence" and an ability to "understand every word I say". The complexity of cetacean societies is another point frequently cited, but ants and bees, for example, have indisputably complex societies and we do not usually acknowledge these creatures as highly "intelligent". What about the cetacean's "sophisticated communication abilities"? We still know very little about the social significance of many of their sounds (excluding echolocation, which is only an aid for hunting and exploring the environment), body language and other communication systems, but in general the repertoire is far too limited to provide anything like our kind of "language". Experiments have shown that some dolphins may have the rudimentary skills necessary for understanding and use of language, but these skills seem fairly common, and have so far been found in a range of species including pigeons, pinnipeds and apes. Again, what could be more "sophisticated" than the multiple communication systems of bees? And how do we usually regard bees?

Friendliness and helpfulness towards people are often discussed, but are we flattering ourselves in believing that the animals really "intended" to help? For perhaps obvious reasons we hear less of unhelpful behaviour, but there are well-documented cases. Many species of wild animals have been tamed or habituated to humans. Sometimes such animals become a danger to themselves or to people. Even tamed wild dolphins can become a considerable nuisance (for example setting boats adrift by pulling up anchors) and sometimes dangerous. Instances of "friendly" dolphins attacking swimmers (apparently unprovoked) are well documented, as are instances of swimmers being pushed out to sea, "abducted" or prevented from re-entering boats and other craft (e.g. Lockyer, 1990).

Gaskin (1982) has concluded that there is abundant evidence that cetaceans communicate information about "what", "where" and "who". There is no substantive evidence that they transmit information about "when", "how" or "why". So with respect to Kipling's (1902) "six honest serving men" of learning and intellect, cetaceans appear to be three servants short.

Conclusion

There is another—less anthropomorphic or "speciesist"—way of looking at the question of general "intelligence". All living species must be highly "intelligent" in a broad sense in order to survive. From this point of view, humans are no more and no less than one of the species living on this planet with particular adaptations (specialised "intelligence") for their own way of life. This perspective allows us to view the superb professionalism of all species with equal respect, and not in some artificial ranking order of higher or lower "intelligence" (with the hidden assumption that they are more or less worthy of conservation and consideration, and that as humans are, of course, in the first rank, their wishes have priority).

Dawkins (1980) recognises that suffering in animals may be difficult to measure and that misinterpretations of the meaning of animal behaviour can arise from projecting human feelings on to animals. Being "human-like" or "higher" or "more intelligent" is considered a poor guide to whether an animal experiences suffering. Behavioural and physiological evidence are more reliable and, taken together with information on the treatment of the animals, the situation can be evaluated. Without this basic preparation, suffering may be seen where there is none or, worse, may be overlooked because it does not wear a human face.

Thus, while it is not yet possible to make any final scientific judgements on cetacean "intelligence", there are sufficient doubts to render the unqualified perpetuation of the dogma highly questionable—and possibly even counter-productive in the wider conservation and animal welfare context.

References

Allison, T., Van Twyner, H. and Goff, W.H. (1972). Electrophysiological studies of the echidna, *Tachyglossus aculeatus*. I. Waking and sleep. *Arch. ital. biol.* 110: 145–184.

Crick, F. and Mitchison, G. (1983). The function of dream sleep. *Nature* 304: 111–114.

Dawkins, M.S. (1980). *Animal Suffering*. Chapman and Hall, London. 1980

Defran, R.H. and Pryor, K. (1980). The behaviour and training of cetaceans in captivity. pp. 319–362. In: L.M. Herman (Ed.) *Cetacean Behaviour: Mechanisms and Functions*. John Wiley and Sons, New York. 463 pp.

Garey, L.J. and Revishchin, A.V. (1990). Structure and thalamocortical relations of the cetacean sensory cortex: histological, tracer and immunocytochemical studies. pp. 19–30 In: J.A. Thomas and R.A. Kastelein (Eds) *Sensory Abilities of Cetaceans: Laboratory and Field Evidence*. Plenum Press, New York. 710 pp.

Gaskin, D.E. (1982). *The Ecology of Whales and Dolphins*. Heinemann, London. 459 pp.

Glazer, I.I., Morgane, P.J. and Leranth, C. (1990). Immunocytochemistry of neurotransmitters in visual neocortex of several toothed whales: light and electron microscope study. p. 39–66 In: J.A. Thomas and R.A. Kastelein (Eds) *Sensory Abilities of Cetaceans: Laboratory and Field Evidence*. Plenum Press, New York. 710 pp.

Hahn, M.E., Jensen, C. and Dudek, B.C. (Eds) (1979). *Development and Evolution of Brain Size. Behavioral Implications*. Academic Press, New York. 393 pp.

Harlow, H.F. (1949). The formation of learning sets. *Psychol. Rev.* 56: 51–65.

Holloway, R.L. (1979). Brain size, allometry and reorganization: toward a synthesis. p. 59–88. In: Hahn, M.E., Jensen, C. and Dudek, B.C. (Eds) *Development and Evolution of Brain*

Size. Behavioral Implications. Academic Press, New York. 393 pp.

Jerison, H.J. (1978). Brain and intelligence in whales. p. 159–197. In: *Whales and Whaling*. Australian Government Publishing Service, Canberra. Vol. 2. 219 pp.

Jerison, H.J. (1979) The evolution of diversity in brain size. p. 29–57. In: Hahn, M.E., Jensen, C. and Dudek, B.C. (Eds) *Development and Evolution of Brain Size. Behavioral Implications*. Academic Press, New York. 393 pp.

Kesarev, V.S., Malofeyeva, L.I. and Trykova, O.V. (1977). Ecological specificity of cetacean neocortex. *J. Hirnforsch.* 18: 447–460.

Kipling, R. (1902). *Just-So Stories*. Macmillan and Co. Ltd., London.

Kuhlenbeck, H. (1978). *The Central Nervous System of Vertebrates. Vol. 5: Part II. Mammalian Telencephalon: Surface Morphology and Cerebral Cortex—The Vertebrate Neuroaxis as a Whole*. Karger, Basle. 636 pp.

Lilly, J.C. (1967). *The Mind of the Dolphin*. Doubleday, New York.

Lockyer, C. (1990). Review of incidents involving wild, sociable dolphins, worldwide. PP. 337–353 In: S. Leatherwood and R.R. Reeves (Eds) *The Bottlenose Dolphin*. Academic Press, San Diego. 653 pp.

Macphail, E.M. (1982). *Brain and Intelligence in Vertebrates*. Clarendon Press, Oxford. 433 pp.

Morgane, P.J., Jacobs, M.S. and Galaburda, A. (1986). Evolutionary morphology of the dolphin brain. pp. 5–29. In: Schusterman, R.J., Thomas, J.A. and Wood, F.G. (Eds) *Dolphin Cognition and Behaviour: A Comparative Approach*. Lawrence Erlbaum and Associates, London. 393 pp.

Mukhametov, L.M. (1984). Sleep in marine mammals. pp. 227–237. In: A. Borbely and J-L. Valatax (Eds) *Sleep Mechanisms*. Experimental Brain Research. Suppl. 8. Springer-Verlag, Berlin.

Pilleri, G., Gihr, M. and Kraus, C. (1985). Cephalization in rodents with particular reference to the Canadian beaver

(*Castor canadensis*). pp. 11–102. In: G. Pilleri (Ed.) *Investigations on Beavers IV*. Berne, Switzerland.

Ridgway, S.H. (1986). Dolphin brain size. PP. 59–70 In: M.M. Bryden and R.J. Harrison (Eds) *Research on Dolphins*. Clarendon Press, Oxford. 478 pp.

Supin, A. Ya., Mukhametov, L.M., Ladygina, T.F., Popov, V.V., Mass, A.M. and Poliakova, I.G. (1978). *Electrophysiological Investigation of the Dolphin Brain*. Nauka, Moscow. 213 pp.

Why Whale?

Do Ecology and Common Sense Provide Any Answers?

MILTON FREEMAN

Canadian Circumpolar Institute

University of Alberta, Edmonton

This paper could as relevantly have been entitled "Why *not* Whale?". However, that particular title would likely appear unnecessarily provocative or even offensive to some individuals, and as such would be damaging to the more useful, constructive, exchange of ideas needed at this time in discussions about whales and whaling.

Nevertheless, having suggested that the title "Why Not Whale?" is a quite valid one, some explanation might be in order. First some background.

Canada is a vast geographically and culturally varied country whose east coast is ice-infested for several months of the year, and whose considerably more extensive northern coastline is ice free for only a few weeks of the year. Most Canadians are well aware that these sparsely occupied climatically-extreme reaches of the country are quite incapable of supporting agriculture, nor indeed few other economic or industrial means of livelihood. As a consequence, in such locations distinctive cultures and forms of meaningful social existence have come to depend upon utilizing the renewable resources found in these expansive northern regions.

In the Arctic certainly, and arguably in most sub-Arctic coastal areas also, despite the ice-covered seas for much of the year, the valuable resources, representing the real wealth of the region, are the living marine resources

The Nature of Cold-Region Marine Ecosystems

It is an ecological fact that cold-water marine ecosystems are different in all sorts of important respects from temperate zone or warm-water systems further to the south (Dunbar 1968). Furthermore, in relation to the topic under discussion here, one important feature to note is the relative lack of species of fin fishes, and the relative abundance and diversity of warm-blooded marine species (Freeman 1984;1988a; 1988b). Thus in the polar regions a diverse assemblage of mammals and birds occupy the ecological niches that a large number of fish species would ordinarily be expected to occupy in temperate or warmer waters. In the colder waters, instead of vast shoals of herring skimming off the plankton, there are large-bodied whales skimming off the plankton. Instead of larger fish eating smaller fish, there are seals or small whales eating the small fish.

People living in these cold-water regions naturally base their economies and diets heavily upon these large-bodied marine resources, and have done so since the beginning of human occupation in the region (McCartney 1984). Hunting people are adaptive, they are inventive, they have to be to stay alive in a region where things can go wrong at any time (and frequently do!). So it presents no great challenge to devise ways to harvest these sea mammals successfully. Consequently, many people in the circumpolar regions (and some of those living just outside those regions, but seasonally moving north to harvest the resources) base their economy on the wealth of these cold water ecosystems so abundantly supplied with diverse marine mammals: the large whales (such as the bowhead, gray, fin, humpback, or sei) the medium-sized minke, killer, beaked, bottlenose and pilot whales, and the numerous small cetaceans (such as beluga, narwhal and various dolphins and porpoises) and the walrus and several species of seal (Freeman 1984).

Hunting societies, in elaborating their economic systems, and because of the integrated nature of human social and cultural arrangements, develop complex human-environmental inter-dependencies focused upon the important resource species. For example, there are appropriate technologies (including an extensive body of traditional knowledge) and ritual obser-vances elaborated for particular harvesting activities, there are appropriate systems for ensuring social cohesion and co-oper-ation, of assigning status and prestige and leadership, rules for decision-making, whether in the political or purely social con-text, in short, complex socio-cultural systems having a depen-dent relationship upon the underlying resource utilizing prac-tices of these distinctive coastal societies.

Without going further into this, it is apparent why, in regard to any consideration of human societies occupying the cold ocean areas of the globe, the question to ask is "Why *not* Whale?"—it all makes so much ecological sense and is, in every way, an entirely rational adaptation given the relative ease with which skilled hunters can catch whales and the large amount of nourishing food, fuel and fabricational materials each of these animals provide.

The Question of Ethics

Presumably there are reasons put forward by opponents of whaling why people today should not whale, even when con-tinuing dependencies based upon ecology, geography, econom-ics and tradition make it so obvious a choice. One reason being advanced today is that there are ethical reasons not to whale.

With regard to the question of ethics, it seems perfectly rea-sonable to believe that humankind has a moral obligation to avoid treating animals with cruelty. However, holding that belief does not, of itself, make animals the moral equal of humans.

From this it follows that we are under no moral obligations to not use animals for our own purposes for food, for various other commercial purposes, for sport or for increasing our knowledge about the world (in other words, in scientific investigations). Adopting such an ethical stance concerning responsible use however, in no way reduces our obligation to avoid inflicting cruelty upon animals.

If a given act is not prohibited by a moral imperative, then it is morally permissible, and since the use of animals as human food or for commerce is not morally prohibited, then killing animals (such as whales) for food or trade is a perfectly moral act. But as stated earlier, wantonly inflicting pain on another species *is* a wrongful act, and causing any kind of suffering must in general be justified. So ethical individuals are concerned to treat animals humanely, to avoid cruelty at all times. Those opposing the use of whales for food declare that whaling constitutes cruel and inhumane behaviour, and for this reason whaling should be prohibited.

The Question of Cruel and Inhumane Treatment of Animals

According to the Oxford or Webster's dictionaries, the terms inhumane and cruel are defined as follows:

> **Inhumane:** devoid of compassion, sympathy or consideration; lacking the qualities mercy, pity, kindness or tenderness; barbarous, cruel, savage.
> **Cruel:** disposed to inflict pain in a wanton, vindictive manner; pleased by hurting another; sadistic; devoid of kindness; hard-hearted; pitiless.

Scientists, government officials and many others having personal knowledge of hunters and whalers in the Arctic and in other countries, would likely be the first to attest that the behaviour and nature of individual whalers they know does not fit the qualities outlined in the categories "cruel" and "inhumane", despite the image whalers have been given through the writing of journalists and others supporting, for whatever reason, an end to whaling. Each year numbers of whalers, from the United States, Canada, Greenland, Norway, Iceland and Japan attend the IWC meetings, so non whalers (including members of national delegations and journalists) attending these meetings can easily judge for themselves how well theses designations can reasonably be applied to the individuals who practice whaling as a profession. In addition to first hand encounters with whalers, an extensive scientific literature now exists thoroughly documenting the extent to which whaling in various coastal societies supports important socio-cultural institutions and is itself supported by a complex system of religious and ideological traditions, such that whalers cannot, by any reasonable stretch of the imagination be thought of as lacking concern for the species of animal they hunt (e.g. Worl 1980; Bockstoce *et al.* 1982; Akimichi *et al.* 1988; Braund *et al.* 1989; Manderson and Hardacre 1989; Kalland 1990)

However, even if it were to be allowed that whalers are not themselves inhumane or cruel people, could it not be argued that the act of whaling itself is cruel and inhumane? Critical examination of that charge requires to be made.

Coming to Terms with the Need to Kill for Food

Anthropologists in particular are well aware of how hunters (including whalers) have to make serious, conscious, efforts to come to terms with the demands of their profession. A famous

Inuit hunter in the Arctic is quoted as saying that "the greatest peril of life lies in the fact that human food consists entirely of souls" (Rasmussen 1929:56). In other words, it is a troubling fact that to sustain life, one has to take life. the souls of animals needed to be taken as food are just as in humans, and must be propitiated: "lest they should revenge themselves on us for taking away their bodies" (*ibid*) . Thus whaling in the Arctic, as in some other regions, is associated with many formal rules, ceremonies and ritual observances (Worl 1980; Bockstoce *et al.* 1982). A contemporary Alaskan whaler, Patrick Attungana, is quoted in a recent Alaskan magazine as saying:

> Our body fluids are mixed with the blood of animals ... the Inupiat, the whiteman and the animals have one breath. All three have one source of living. When the whale is caught, just the body dies, but the whole whale gives itself to all the people. The whale being or spirit goes into the bladder, and the whaler who catches the whale removes the bladder ... and brings it to his village. Those whales who stop in each of the whaling villages, their whale being or spirit never dies ... when (the whalers) get to the camp, the dead whale's spirit returns to the live whales. He tells them that his hosts were good to him.

For similar reasons of concern, Japanese whalers surround their whaling activities with religious ceremonies and rites, both for the purification of their boats and hunting equipment, and for the peaceful repose of the souls of the whales they anticipate killing and subsequently kill (Akimichi *et al.* 1988: 52–65; Kalland and Moeran 1990: 151–159).

These observances do not suggest a lack of consideration, compassion or concern for the whales, which is what the charge of the "inhumaneness" wold require to be sustained.

A few years ago at the IWC, a member of the Alaskan Eskimo Whaling Commission pleaded with the members of the

Aboriginal Whaling Subcommittee to stop speaking of the "inhumaneness" of the Eskimo whale hunt—it is, by its very practice and contemplation anything but inhumane, if that term is used correctly. It should be also noted that in recent years the Alaskan Eskimo Whaling Commission has undertaken considerable research on adapting the penthrite grenade to the hand held whaling lances and shoulder guns used in the bowhead whale hunt. This research has the dual objectives of not only improving hunting efficiency but also of addressing the concerns of those people who wish to see whale killing methods approach the ideal of achieving the quickest possible death during hunting.

The penthrite charge referred to above is a much improved means of killing whales, compared to the earlier black powder explosive grenade and the still earlier (but now unused) non exploding (cold) harpoon. Whereas the former exploding grenade killed by laceration, and only in the case of a lethally-placed shot near the heart or brain was dead instant, the penthrite charge is a means of transmitting a stunning shock to the central nervous system, so that almost every hit ensures unconsciousness followed by very speedy death. In some cases, as in the Japanese fishery, those whales not killed instantly, are within seconds drawn along the catcher boats and electrocuted.

Whose Ethical Standards?

Another aspect of the ethics argument we must briefly consider is: whose ethical standards are to be applied when dealing with international, and hence intercultural, debate. It is currently fashionable to think of animal rights or environmental rights as being very enlightened, and therefore the current standard for judging our treatment of nature.

However, the issue is far more confused than it is straight forward. For example, in 1979 a U.S. study found that more then three out of four Americans accepted whaling, provided that the fishery did not threaten the species with extinction and that the hunt served useful purposes (Kellert 1979). Presumably, providing food, jobs and human health and well-being all qualify as "useful purposes". A similar public opinion poll, carried out in Australia at about the same time, likewise found majority of respondents could accept a continuation of whaling. When Australians were asked in a national poll conducted by the Australian Conservation Foundation to choose between the following two options:

> should whales be killed at all, even if it could be shown that whaling does not threaten the existence of the species

OR

Whaling should be continued on a controlled basis

the majority (by a plurality of almost 25 percent) answered that whaling should be continued on a controlled basis (Frost 1978:326).

These American and Australian poll results were obtained during the very height of highly publicized campaigns to "Save the Whales", when very great efforts were underway to try and persuade people that continued hunting would lead to the imminent extinction of the "whale species". These persuasive advertising campaigns and lobbying efforts, "many of which were more passionate than informative" (Aron 1988:108), though apparently not influencing most of the public, certainly caused (and apparently still cause) politicians to consider the matter as being one of major public concern.

At the present time Save the Whales movement continues to

have value to its proponents, who include animal welfare and animal rights groups as well as some environmental organizations and those dedicated to the contemplation of whales. As advocating the non consumptive values of whales confers financial and political clout to its proponents these campaigns will persist, only ceasing when the issue, the movement and those promoting it are better understood by the public and politicians.

In the meantime, countries that no longer require to engage in whaling, and whose citizens are believed (perhaps erroneously, if the findings of the Kellert and Frost studies (op. cit.) are any indication) to support an end to whaling in their own countries, should certainly not feel that this gives them any moral right to impose their particular circumstances or view of propriety on to other countries that may, because of their history, culture of ecological circumstance be required to follow different sustainable resource use practices. William Aron, when writing of U.S. legislators' concern for whale protection warned: "we must clearly recognize that there is a difference between imposing a moral or ethical standard on (our own) citizens and imposing such standards on the international community" (Aron 1988:107).

Furthermore, in regard to animal welfare concerns, it should be remembered that these high ethical ideals are very selective applied in practice, for there are a vast number of everyday uses of animals that are, by many peoples' standards, totally unacceptable. I refer here to the caging of animals in zoos, pet shops and factory farms, performing animals in circuses or rodeos, the unlicensed and unsupervised keeping of all sorts of animals as pets, often by thoughtless and uninformed people (some of whom know or learn how to look after an animal, others of whom, sadly, do not).

Is it possible that we urban dwellers have a vast collective guilt about the human treatment of animals, a vague unease about what transpired before that nice juicy steak arrives sizzling on the plate and gives us so much pleasure in the contemplating and then the eating? Remember, that to some of the people who protest against whaling, eating a beef steak is equally unacceptable behaviour, according to their particular ethical standards.

The Uneven Application of Ethical Concern

It is important to realize that in Western Europe, North America and some other societies, a selective morality applies toward animals. It seems that the campaigns of many animal rights and environmental organizations direct our attention and sympathy toward some animal species rather than to others. For example, all primate species, cats, dogs, seals, whales, dolphins and elephants, sometimes horses and donkeys also, are certainly among the favoured species. It is much harder to muster sympathy for a snake or even a small mammal (especially if it has a long hairless tail, a rat-like head and sharp teeth).

When concern is expressed about "whales" (as a generic category), attention is focused upon one of a class of animals that have been variously referred to as the "CM animals", the *Charismatic Megafauna* species, or the *Phenomenologically Significant Animals.* Harp seal pups, most whales and dolphins, pandas, elephants, are all a '10' on a scale of 1–10, so to argue against the strong emotional feelings the public has against killing such appealing animals is almost impossible, no matter how rational the arguments may be. Certain sorts of animals it seems, are easily placed by the public into non-use categories. The reason for this ease of elevations to protected non-use status is because as species they tend to be photogenic, or in reality *mediagenic* in attracting the media and the public alike.

The mediagenic animals have become important symbols for

urban people, who feel genuine concern for what they believe is being done to the natural environment due in good measure to the demands of an urban, industrial, lifestyle which, *inter alia*, destroys wild places and the animals and plants inhabiting them. Indeed, it has been reliably reported that during the last two decades of the present century about one-fifth of the species on earth may disappear (Brown 1991:51). Relevant to our concerns here, is the observation that marine mammals are among the least threatened groups of animals when considered in the global context (Clark 1989:51)

Many of these concerned urban-dwellers never see or experience wilderness or exotic species in the wild, they just see symbolic or photographic representations—on TV, in magazines or in picture books. It is the power of these representations, these graphic symbols, in some individuals vicariously reinforced by an infrequent eco-tour or vacation to a significant and magnificent natural area, that causes the desire, often bordering on an intense felt need, to do something to preserve the symbol that has come to mean so much. And there are plenty of people to help the concerned individual to actually do something: lobbyists and advocates, willing to do battle on the individual's behalf against the government or whoever is in charge, to save this, that, or the other significant natural resource.

At first sight it might appear paradoxical, sending one's own money to non-governmental organizations, when there are professionals working in government, paid by hard-earned tax monies, whose job is is to ensure the environment is protected at no extra charge. Why send money to your favourite animal-saving or symbol-promoting group? Why not just write your national or local government environment department?

The significant difference between a wildlife agency and an animal protection organization is that the animal protection group focuses attention on saving the *individual* animal—the individual whale or the seal pup, the mother elephant and her calf, whereas the government conservation department is concerned to conserve the population, the biological community, ecologic integrity or balance, but not individual animals. In other words, such government agencies are mandated to engage only in some neutral, impersonal, bland and emotionally unappealing task, in contrast to the much more emotionally-charged mission offered by the alternative non-governmental organization. So a market exists for addressing the general publics' unmet "environmental" and animal welfare concerns, and a growth industry of advocate organizations has come in to existence to address the real or perceived problems the public associates with various visually and symbolically appealing natural resources.

The Ecological Perspective

Unfortunately, peoples' concerns about individual animals are not matched by their understanding of ecological reality. We live in a diverse and complex world, so that simplistic diagnoses of complex questions are not likely to lead to significant improvements. Indeed, they may even be counterproductive in deflecting attention away from more important environmental matters as many concerned environmental scientists are pointing out (e.g. Brownell *et al.* 1989; Tyack 1989). Apart from deflecting limited resources away from more urgent conservation issues, it should also be realized that most successful protest movements, being single-issue oriented (save the seal, save the whale) are, by their very nature, ecologically unsound.

To most people "saving whales" from extinction is equated in their minds with preventing them from being harpooned, a simple-minded notion graphically purveyed by most environmental and animal-saving organizations. Given enough time and no economic restraints, it just might be theoretically possible to wipe out a local population of whales by harpooning, though it should be remembered that industrial-scale whalers and other whalers have been notably unsuccessful in doing that, despite the sometimes predatory excesses of the past.

In the real world, where practical issues tend to determine environmental outcomes, killing off a population of say 70,000 minke whales in the North-east Atlantic could hardly occur by mistake. Indeed, even if a government was somewhat indifferent to the whales, it would take quite a long time to reduce it to dangerously low levels *unless* allowing huge annual harvests, which no government or whaler advocates. A stock of minke whales of this size likely adds a couple of thousand additional whales to its number each year, so harvesting at least some of that production might be considered reasonable fishery practice.

This same minke whale species exists throughout the world's oceans and seas, and numbers in the many hundreds of thousands, "and cannot, in a biological sense, be perceived as (an) endangered species" (Aron 1988:103). At the present time, unlike in years past, the demand for whale oil that fuelled the explosive growth of the whaling industry has, in global terms, completely dried up. The large Antarctic whaling fleets of thirty or forty years ago no longer exist, and even with three-quarters of a million Antarctic minke whales likely producing somewhere between 30–40,000 additional whales per year (after taking account of the 60–80,000 that likely die of natural causes), it's hard to imagine what the financial incentive would be for many to venture into this very specialized commercial arena. To invoke images of thirty or forty years ago when rehabilitating a war-shattered Europe required huge quantities of edible oils, protein and other industrial materials provided by large scale whaling, which is certainly not the case today, is totally misleading.

What threatens sea life most profoundly and damagingly, whether whales, seals, fish or the integrity of the total marine system, is the overloading of these natural systems with chemical pollutants. Removing biomass doesn't seriously threaten the whole system, for natural ecosystems are incredibly complex (even the most apparently simple) and consequently are better characterised as being *resilient* (rather than fragile) to natural perturbations (Dunbar 1985:26–27).

However, much of pollution tends to be unnatural, in the sense of being comprised of new contaminants of anthropogenic origin, so that successful adaptation on the part of species requires time and trial-and-error evolutionary change. Furthermore, such chemical contaminants can be exceedingly harmful as they pose what is called *indiscriminate* stress (i.e. variously impacting all the organisms in a population that is vulnerable to that particular stress).

In marked contrast to indiscriminate stress affecting the population (and perhaps other components of the whole biological community), natural and hunting mortality on the other hand, heavily stresses only a few individuals in a particular population or breeding stock, leaving the remaining members of that population biologically unimpaired.

It should be obvious then, when identifying serious threats to whale stocks (or other marine life), what constitutes the significant negative affects. Indeed, even if we do not know in precise scientific ways what the exact effect is of dumping toxic waste of myriad kinds into the seas of the world we do know it impacts the population as a whole, and that should be of major concern.

A Question of Priorities

We really need to ask of the "save the whale groups", and indeed of the International Whaling Commission itself, "have you got your priorities straight, do have reasoned understanding of where your zeal should be aimed?" There appears to be almost no understanding that the self-interest of the whaling-dependent societies and industries (in today's more enlightened world if not before) is directed toward sustainably using whales as a self-renewing resource.

In the Arctic regions, it is generally recognized by environmental groups—in both Alaska and Canada at least—that local hunters represent the greatest defence against industrial encroachment and resultant damage to critical habitat. On federal lands in northern Canada uranium mines and pipelines, for example, have been kept out of the caribou calving or migratory areas, and away from fish-spawning areas precisely because those living resources are important economic resources to local residents. Indian communities in Alaska and Indian and Invialuit communities in the western Canadian Artic are joined with U.S. and Canadian environmental organizations in opposing the oil exploration proposed for the critical habitat in the Artic National Wildlife Refuge on the Alaskan North Slope; and stringent environmental safeguards are far more likely to be imposed on careless exploration and development of off-shore oil and gas in the Beaufort Sea precisely *because* Inuit hunters harvest bowhead and beluga whales in those areas.

Thus recognizing the economic utility of living resources, at least in some jurisdictions, appears to help in the political process that decides what land and water uses to allow, what environmental trade-offs are acceptable or not.

The human population is projected to increase by another four billion people within the lifetime of many people thinking seriously about the environmental predicament collectively faced today. These billions will for the most part be hungry, restless and desperate. With this prospect in mind it seems not unreasonable to hope that responsible governments and international agencies will adopt policies giving priority to the production of healthy food in environmentally safe ways based upon the principles of sustainable and equitable development.

Unfortunately, despite our modern scientific and technological dexterity, modern agriculture does not appear to provide the means for sustainable food production sufficient for the impending human need:

> (Today) meat production is behind a substantial share of the environmental strains induced by the present global agricultural system... In the extreme case of American beef, producing 1 kilogram of steak requires 5 kilograms of grain and the energy equivalent of 9 litres of gasoline, not to mention the associated soil erosion, water consumption, pesticide and fertilizer runoff, groundwater depletion, and emissions of the greenhouse gas methane (Brown 1991:159).

Whaling under conservative management regimes meets both the need for food, is environmentally safe, energy frugal, supportive of local self-sufficiency and is sustainable (Freeman 1991). For those with the compassionate and balanced vision to see clearly, the time for rational thinking and acting on the whaling issue is now, and not at some indefinite time in the uncertain future.

References

Akimichi, T. *et al.* (1988). Small-type coastal whaling in Japan. Occasional Paper No. 27, Boreal Institute for Northern Studies, Edmonton.

Aron, W. (1988). The commons revisited. Coastal Management 16:99–110.

Bockstoce, J. *et al.* (1982). Report of the Cultural Anthropology Panel. Reports of the International Whaling Commission, Special Issue 4. Cambridge.

Braund, S.R. *et al.* (1989). Contemporary socio-cultural characteristics of Japanese small-type coastal whaling. International Whaling Commission Document TC/41/STW1. Cambridge.

Brown, L.R. *et al.* (1991). State of the World 1991. W.W. Norton, New York.

Brownell, R.L. *et al.* The plight of the "forgotten" whales. Oceanus 32:5–11

Dunbar, M.J. (1968). Ecological development in polar regions. Prentice-Hall, Englewood Cliffs, N.J.

Dunbar, M.J. (1985). The Arctic marine ecosystem, pp. 1–35 in F.R. Engelhardt (editor), Petroleum effects in the Arctic environment. Elsevier, London.

Freeman, M.M.R. (1984). Arctic ecosystems, pp. 36–48 in D.J. Damas and W.C. Sturtevant (editors) Handbook of North American Indians, Volume 5. Smithsonian Institution, Washington D.C.

Freeman, M.M.R. (1988a). The north Pacific ecosystem, pp. 5–17 in H. Okada *et al.* (editors) International symposium on maritime adaptations in the north Pacific. Abashiri, Japan.

Freeman M.M.R. (1988b). Raven's creatures, pp 142–3 in W.W. Fitzhugh and A. Crowell (editors) Crossroads of continents: cultures of Siberia and Alaska. Smithsonian Institution, Washington D.C.

Freeman, M.M.R. (1991). Energy, food security and A.D. 2040: the case for sustainable utilization of whale stocks. Resource Management and Optimization 18:235–246.

Frost, S. (1978). Inquiry into whales and whaling. Canberra, Australia (reprinted as The whaling question, Friends of the Earth, San Francisco, 1979).

Kalland, A. (1990). Whaling and whaling communities in Norway and Japan. North Atlantic Studies 2:170–178.

Kalland, A. and B. Moeran (1990). Endangered culture: Japanese whaling in cultural perspective. Nordic institute for Asian Studies, Copenhagen.

Kellert. S.R. (1979). Public attitudes toward critical wildlife and natural habitat issues: phase I. U.S. Printing Office, Washington D.C.

Manderson L. and H. Hardacre (1989). Small-type coastal whaling in Ayukawa. International Whaling Commission Document IWC/41/SE3, Cambridge.

McCartney, A.P. (1984). History of Native whaling in the Artic and sub-Artic, pp. 79–111 in H.K. s'Jacob *et al.* (editors) Artic whaling. University of Groningen Artic Centre, The Netherlands.

Rasmussen, K. (1929). Intellectual culture of the Hudson Bay Eskimos. Report of the Fifth Thule Expedition 8 (1), 304 pp.

Tyack, P.H. (1989). Lets have less public relations and more ecology. Oceanus 32:103–108.

Worl, R. (1980). The North Slope Inupiat Whaling Complex. Senri Ethnological Studies 4:305–320.